MW01173270

DIARY

My
Personal
Inspirational Book

Prayer -N- Praise Diary

By Deidre Proctor

This Diary Belongs to

_____

If lost, please return to me by contacting me at:

Email: _____

Phone: _____

Prayer -N- Praise Diary

All Scriptures are referenced from https://www.biblegateway.com/ (the King James Version of the Bible).

ISBN: 978-0-9832611-3-1
1st edition, January 2022
Printed in the United States of America

Why Pray -N- Praise?

God loves to fellowship with us. He loves to listen to our hearts and speak to us. As our Father, He expects us to come to Him when we have a care, a worry, or simply just need a little or a lot of help.

"Cast all your anxiety on him because he cares for you" 1 Peter 5:7

He doesn't care if we come to Him in prayer for ourselves or if we are interceding for someone else.

And He is just as pleased to hear our praises. When He answers our prayers, we are to immediately praise him, even if the answer to our prayers was not the answer we were expecting. Or, even if we do not receive an immediate answer. As He showers us with daily mercy and grace, we are to shower him with love and give Him the highest praises daily.

I wrote Pray -N- Praise to give you a place to record your personal prayers and then record the answers to those prayers.

Prayer -N- Praise Diary

Imagine opening a book that lists time and time again where God has blessed you, your family, and people you have prayed for.

This diary is for Ministry Leaders, Prayer Partners, Prayer Warriors, and all God's children who believe He is the answer to their prayers.

Picture this, you have a job interview, and you pray that God gives you that job. A week later, you are told the job is yours. Answered prayer and praise time!

Or you need a car for your family. You pray for a car, go to the car dealership and you could not get it financed. The next day, your church called and said someone just donated a car to the ministry and they are giving it to you. Answered prayer and praise time!

Or you prayed for a single-parent family to obtain housing and find out a month later, that an organization had the perfect place for them. Answered prayer and praise time!

Or you misplaced your car keys and was running late to work. You couldn't find them anywhere, so you asked the Holy Spirit to help you find them. Then all of a sudden you remembered the last place you left them. Keys found, answered prayer, and praise time!

Yes, write down ALL your prayer requests. The small prayers and the big ones. God deserves all the praise!

Reflect back on those answered prayers often. As you do, you will feel the magnitude of His love. You will cry and laugh and remember how hard you prayed and even how you doubted if God would answer your prayers. You will remember those that prayed for you and with you. You will reflect on how great God is because of His mighty works in your life. This diary will help you increase your faith in God and even thirst after Him more.

When you think a prayer is too big for God, just open up your diary and realize He is bigger than any prayer you can ever pray.

How To Use The
Prayer -N- Praise Diary

At the beginning of the day, during the day or before you lay down to sleep, open your diary and write your prayer requests in it. Remember, it does not matter how big or small your prayer is. **It is important to be sure to write the date next to your prayer request.**

After God answers your prayer, go back to your diary and find that prayer. In the Praise Box next to that prayer, write down the date your prayer was answered and praise Him for answering your prayer. Write whatever comes to mind.

On the Note Pages, write down anything else you want to remember about the previous 3 prayers and their praise reports. That could be names of others that were part of your prayer request, more details on how God answered your prayer, or how you felt before and after you submitted your prayer request to God.

Those Note Pages could even become written testimonials for you to share the goodness of your Father with others. Or even a blog!

Prayer -N- Praise Diary

The

Lord's Prayer

"Our Father who is in heaven,
Hallowed be Your name. Your
kingdom come. Your will be done,
On earth as it is in heaven.

Give us this day our daily bread.
And forgive us our debts, as we
also have forgiven our debtors.
And do not lead us into temptation,
but deliver us from evil.

For Yours is the kingdom and the
power and the glory forever. Amen."

My Prayer Requests

My Praise Reports

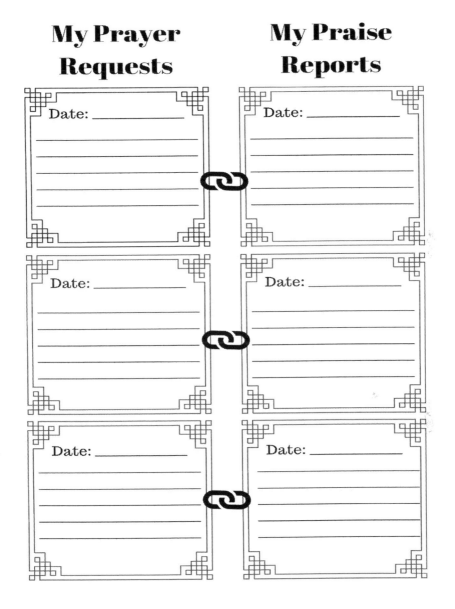

Date: _____

Date: _____

Date: _____

Date: _____

Date: _____

Date: _____

Note Page

_____

_____

_____

_____

_____

_____

_____

_____

_____

_____

_____

_____

_____

_____

_____

_____

_____

_____

_____

_____

_____

_____

_____

_____

_____

_____

My Prayer Requests

My Praise Reports

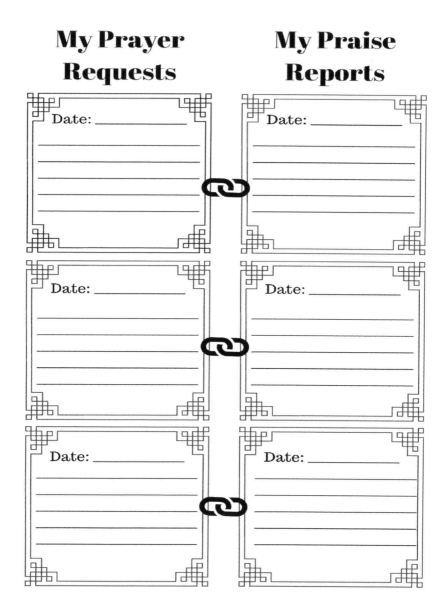

Date: _____

Date: _____

Date: _____

Date: _____

Date: _____

Date: _____

Note Page

_____

_____

_____

_____

_____

_____

_____

_____

_____

_____

_____

_____

Prayer -N- Praise Diary

_____

_____

_____

_____

_____

_____

_____

_____

_____

_____

_____

_____

_____

_____

_____

My Prayer Requests

My Praise Reports

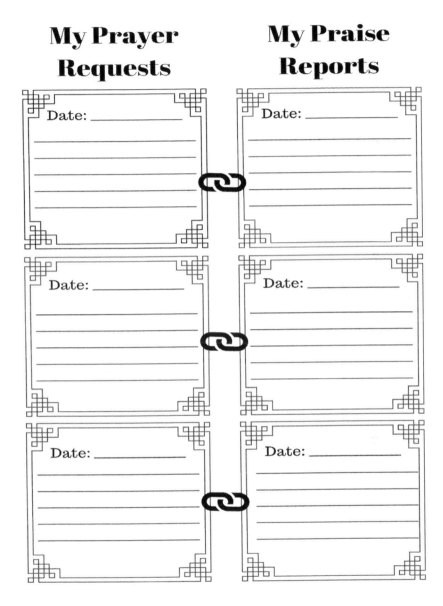

Date: _____

Date: _____

Date: _____

Date: _____

Date: _____

Date: _____

Note Page

_____

_____

_____

_____

_____

_____

_____

_____

_____

_____

_____

_____

_____

Prayer -N- Praise Diary

_____

_____

_____

_____

_____

_____

_____

_____

_____

_____

_____

_____

_____

_____

My Prayer Requests

My Praise Reports

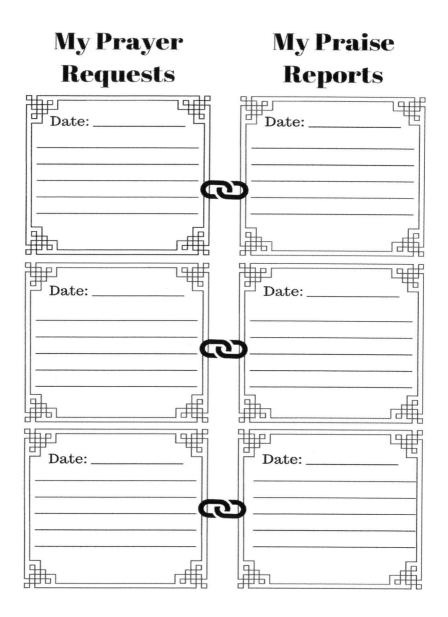

Date: _____

Date: _____

Date: _____

Date: _____

Date: _____

Date: _____

Note Page

_____

_____

_____

_____

_____

_____

_____

_____

_____

_____

_____

_____

_____

_____

_____

_____

_____

_____

_____

_____

_____

_____

_____

_____

_____

_____

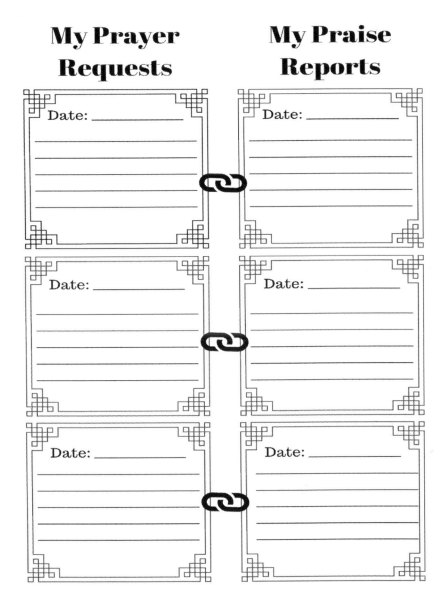

My Prayer Requests

My Praise Reports

Date: _____

Date: _____

Date: _____

Date: _____

Date: _____

Date: _____

Note Page

_____
_____
_____
_____
_____
_____
_____
_____
_____
_____
_____
_____

_____

_____

_____

_____

_____

_____

_____

_____

_____

_____

_____

_____

_____

_____

_____

_____

Philippians 4:6-7

"Be anxious for nothing, but in everything by prayer and supplication with thanksgiving let your requests be made known to God. And the peace of God, which surpasses all comprehension, will guard your hearts and your minds in Christ Jesus."

GALATIANS 5:22-23

JOY & FAITHFULNESS

Goodness

Kindness

Self-Control

Patience

Peace

LOVE

Gentleness

My Prayer Requests

My Praise Reports

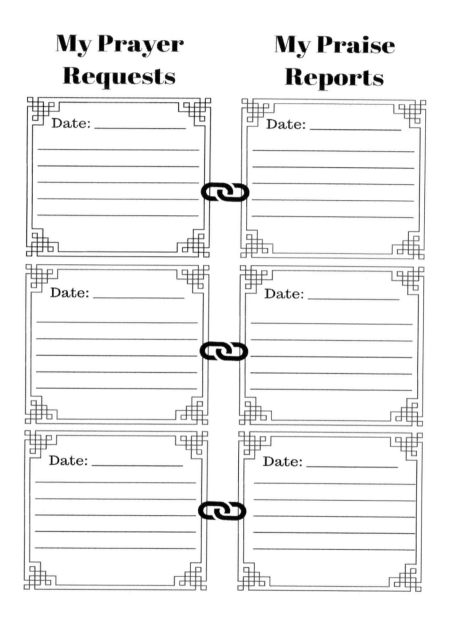

Date: _____

Date: _____

Date: _____

Date: _____

Date: _____

Date: _____

Note Page

_____

_____

_____

_____

_____

_____

_____

_____

_____

_____

_____

_____

_____

_____

_____

_____

_____

_____

_____

_____

_____

_____

_____

_____

_____

_____

_____

_____

My Prayer Requests

My Praise Reports

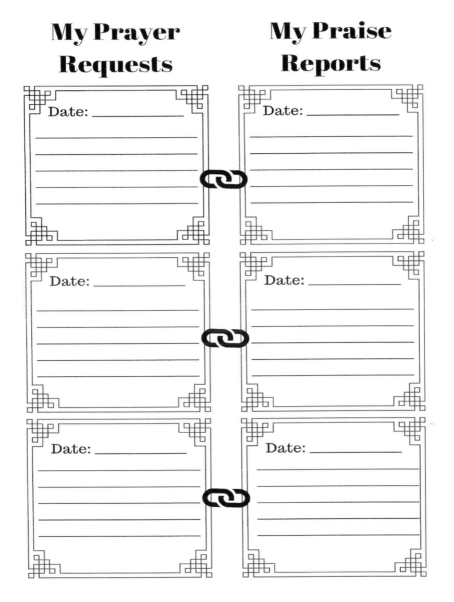

Date: _____

Date: _____

Date: _____

Date: _____

Date: _____

Date: _____

Note Page

_____

_____

_____

_____

_____

_____

_____

_____

_____

_____

_____

_____

_____

Prayer -N- Praise Diary

_____

_____

_____

_____

_____

_____

_____

_____

_____

_____

_____

_____

_____

_____

My Prayer Requests

My Praise Reports

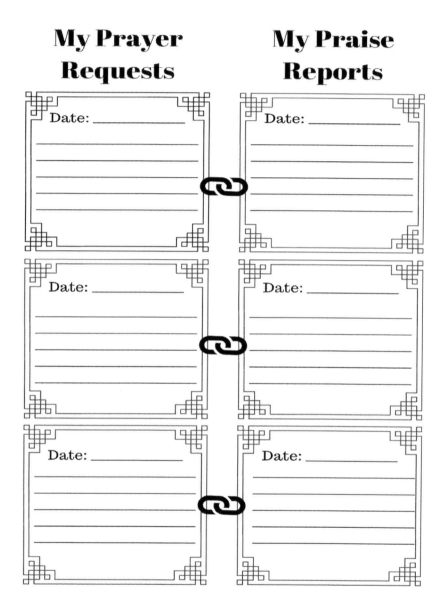

Date: _____

Date: _____

Date: _____

Date: _____

Date: _____

Date: _____

Note Page

_____

_____

_____

_____

_____

_____

_____

_____

_____

_____

_____

_____

_____

Prayer -N- Praise Diary

_____

_____

_____

_____

_____

_____

_____

_____

_____

_____

_____

_____

_____

_____

_____

My Prayer Requests

My Praise Reports

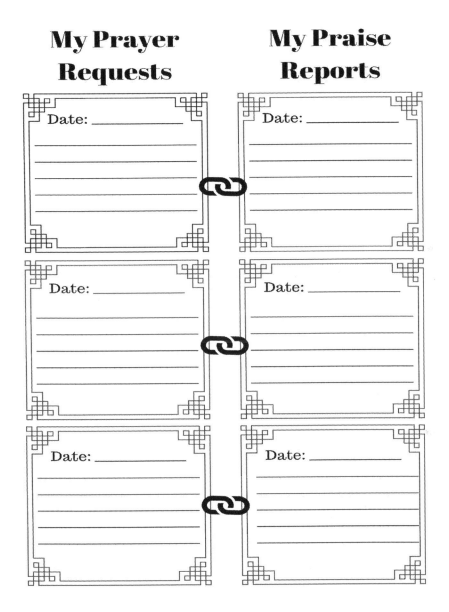

Date: _____

Date: _____

Date: _____

Date: _____

Date: _____

Date: _____

Note Page

_____

_____

_____

_____

_____

_____

_____

_____

_____

_____

_____

_____

_____

_____

_____

_____

_____

_____

_____

_____

_____

_____

_____

_____

_____

_____

_____

_____

My Prayer Requests

My Praise Reports

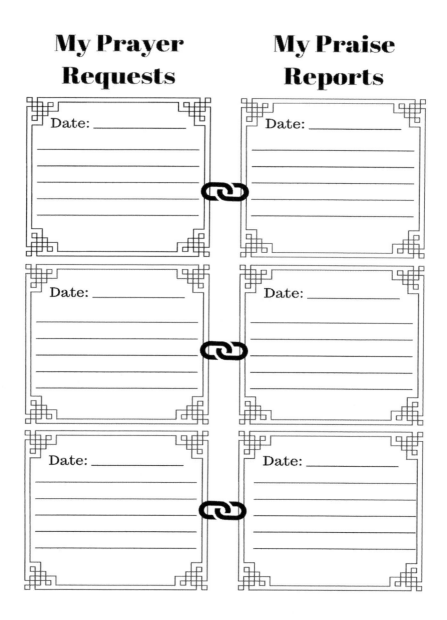

Date: _____

Date: _____

Date: _____

Date: _____

Date: _____

Date: _____

Note Page

_____

_____

_____

_____

_____

_____

_____

_____

_____

_____

_____

_____

_____

_____

_____

_____

_____

_____

_____

_____

_____

_____

_____

_____

_____

_____

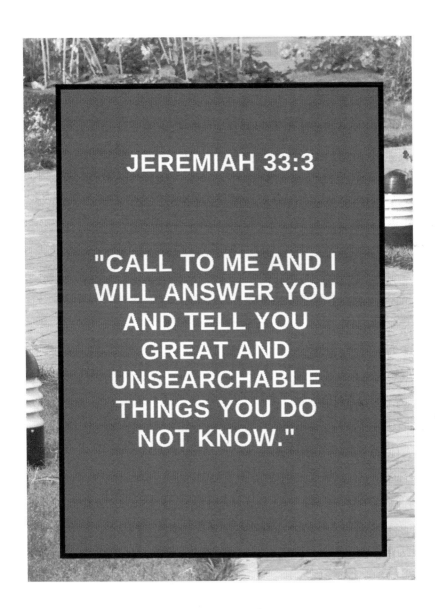

Prayer -N- Praise

What is your favorite praise song?

_____

_____

_____

_____

My Prayer Requests

My Praise Reports

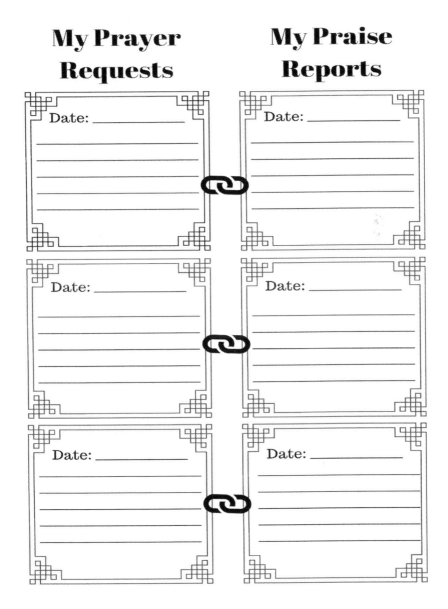

Date: _____

Date: _____

Date: _____

Date: _____

Date: _____

Date: _____

Note Page

_____

_____

_____

_____

_____

_____

_____

_____

_____

_____

_____

_____

_____

_____

_____

My Prayer Requests

My Praise Reports

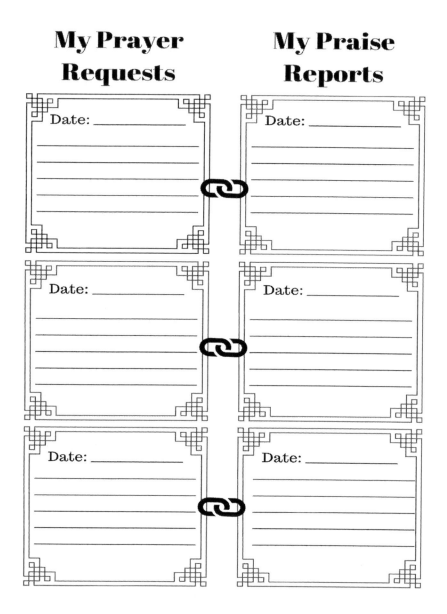

Date: _____

Date: _____

Date: _____

Date: _____

Date: _____

Date: _____

Note Page

_____

_____

_____

_____

_____

_____

_____

_____

_____

_____

_____

_____

_____

Prayer -N- Praise Diary

_____

_____

_____

_____

_____

_____

_____

_____

_____

_____

_____

_____

_____

_____

_____

My Prayer Requests

My Praise Reports

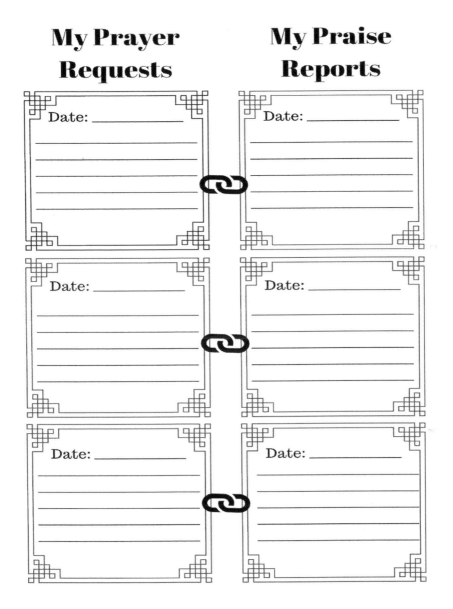

Date: _____

Date: _____

Date: _____

Date: _____

Date: _____

Date: _____

Prayer -N- Praise Diary

Note Page

_____

_____

_____

_____

_____

_____

_____

_____

_____

_____

_____

_____

_____

_____

_____

_____

_____

_____

_____

_____

_____

_____

_____

_____

_____

_____

_____

_____

My Prayer Requests

My Praise Reports

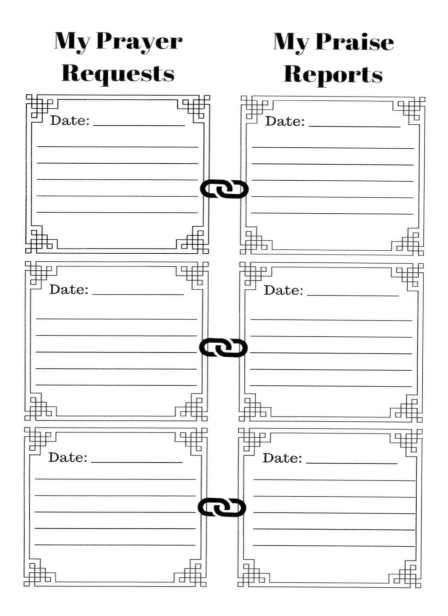

Date: _____

Date: _____

Date: _____

Date: _____

Date: _____

Date: _____

Note Page

_____

_____

_____

_____

_____

_____

_____

_____

_____

_____

_____

_____

_____

_____

_____

_____

_____

_____

_____

_____

_____

_____

_____

_____

_____

_____

_____

My Prayer Requests

My Praise Reports

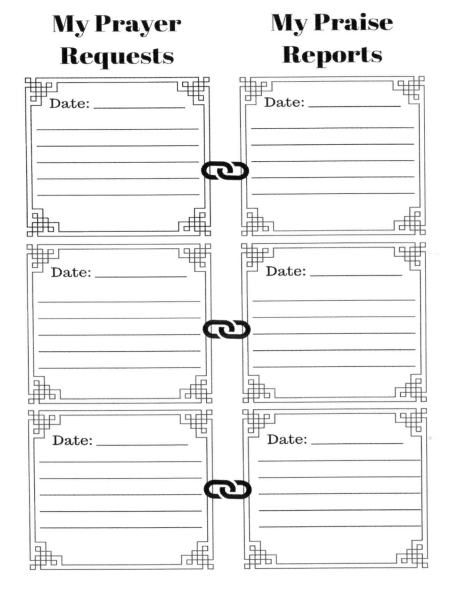

Date: _____

Date: _____

Date: _____

Date: _____

Date: _____

Date: _____

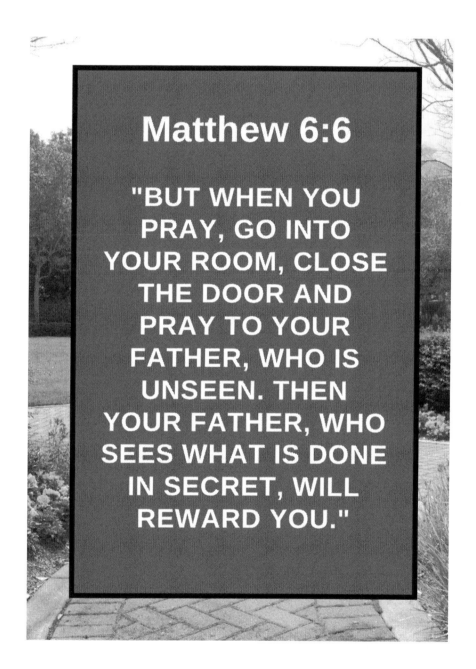

Matthew 6:6

"BUT WHEN YOU PRAY, GO INTO YOUR ROOM, CLOSE THE DOOR AND PRAY TO YOUR FATHER, WHO IS UNSEEN. THEN YOUR FATHER, WHO SEES WHAT IS DONE IN SECRET, WILL REWARD YOU."

How can you be a light in someone's life today:

_____

_____

_____

_____

My Prayer Requests

My Praise Reports

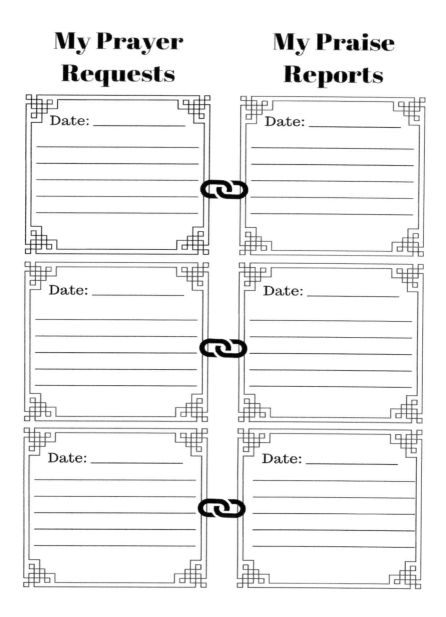

Date: _____

Date: _____

Date: _____

Date: _____

Date: _____

Date: _____

Note Page

_____

_____

_____

_____

_____

_____

_____

_____

_____

_____

_____

_____

_____

_____

_____

_____

_____

_____

_____

_____

_____

_____

_____

_____

_____

_____

_____

_____

My Prayer Requests

My Praise Reports

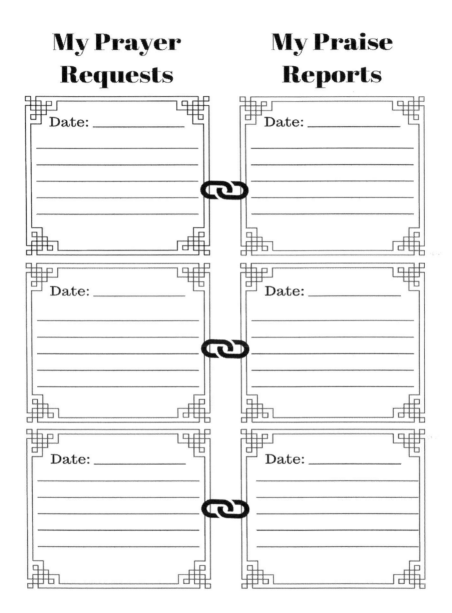

Date: _____

Date: _____

Date: _____

Date: _____

Date: _____

Date: _____

Note Page

_____

_____

_____

_____

_____

_____

_____

_____

_____

_____

_____

_____

Prayer -N- Praise Diary

_____

_____

_____

_____

_____

_____

_____

_____

_____

_____

_____

_____

_____

_____

_____

_____

My Prayer Requests

My Praise Reports

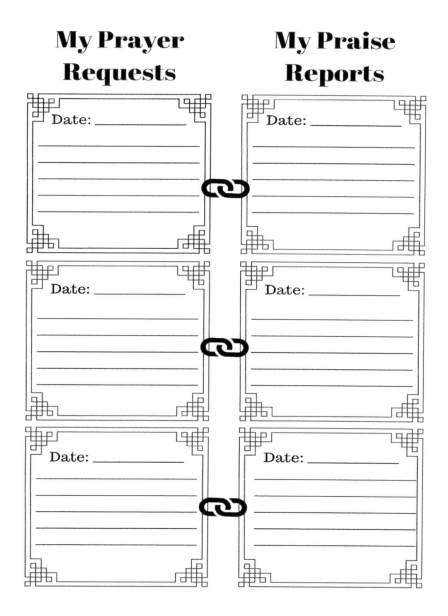

Date: _____

_____
_____
_____
_____

Date: _____

_____
_____
_____
_____

Date: _____

_____
_____
_____
_____

Date: _____

_____
_____
_____
_____

Date: _____

_____
_____
_____
_____

Date: _____

_____
_____
_____
_____

Note Page

_____

_____

_____

_____

_____

_____

_____

_____

_____

_____

_____

_____

_____

My Prayer Requests

My Praise Reports

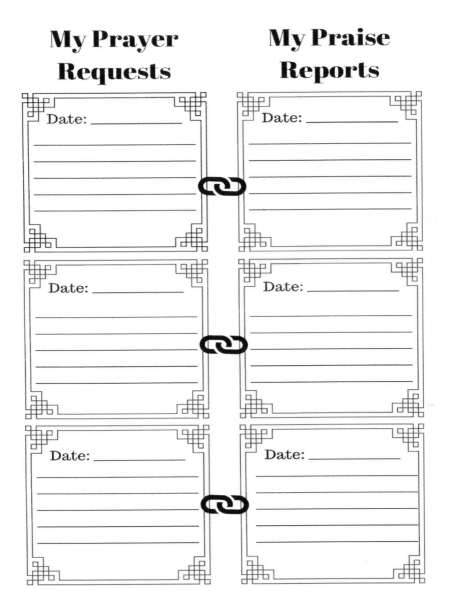

Date: _____

Date: _____

Date: _____

Date: _____

Date: _____

Date: _____

Note Page

_____

_____

_____

_____

_____

_____

_____

_____

_____

_____

_____

_____

Prayer -N- Praise Diary

_____

_____

_____

_____

_____

_____

_____

_____

_____

_____

_____

_____

_____

_____

My Prayer Requests

My Praise Reports

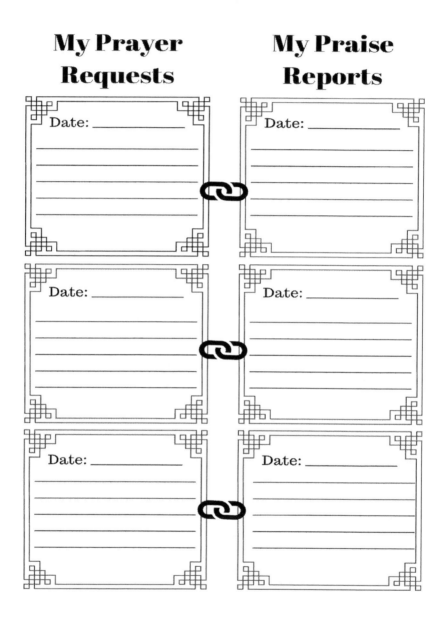

Date: _____

_____
_____
_____
_____

Date: _____

_____
_____
_____
_____

Date: _____

_____
_____
_____
_____

Date: _____

_____
_____
_____
_____

Date: _____

_____
_____
_____
_____

Date: _____

_____
_____
_____
_____

Note Page

_____

_____

_____

_____

_____

_____

_____

_____

_____

_____

_____

_____

_____

_____

_____

_____

_____

_____

_____

_____

_____

_____

_____

_____

_____

_____

_____

_____

_____

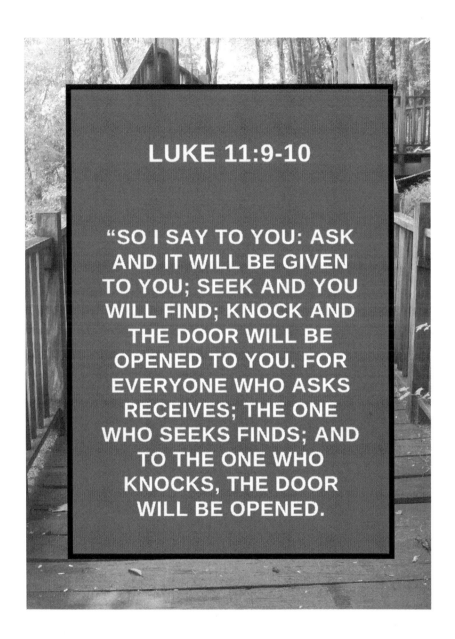

LUKE 11:9-10

"SO I SAY TO YOU: ASK AND IT WILL BE GIVEN TO YOU; SEEK AND YOU WILL FIND; KNOCK AND THE DOOR WILL BE OPENED TO YOU. FOR EVERYONE WHO ASKS RECEIVES; THE ONE WHO SEEKS FINDS; AND TO THE ONE WHO KNOCKS, THE DOOR WILL BE OPENED.

Name one thing you are grateful for today:

_____

_____

_____

_____

My Prayer Requests / My Praise Reports

Date: _____ (x6)

Note Page

_____

_____

_____

_____

_____

_____

_____

_____

_____

_____

_____

_____

_____

My Prayer Requests

My Praise Reports

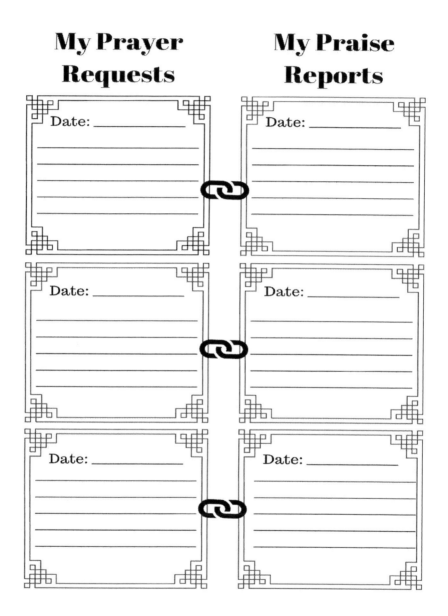

Date: _____

_____
_____
_____
_____
_____

Date: _____

_____
_____
_____
_____
_____

Date: _____

_____
_____
_____
_____
_____

Date: _____

_____
_____
_____
_____
_____

Date: _____

_____
_____
_____
_____
_____

Date: _____

_____
_____
_____
_____
_____

Note Page

_____

_____

_____

_____

_____

_____

_____

_____

_____

_____

_____

_____

My Prayer Requests

My Praise Reports

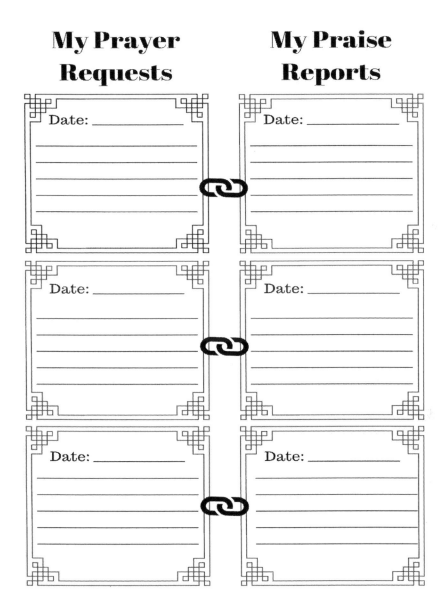

Date: _____

Date: _____

Date: _____

Date: _____

Date: _____

Date: _____

Note Page

_____

_____

_____

_____

_____

_____

_____

_____

_____

_____

_____

_____

_____

_____

_____

_____

_____

_____

_____

_____

_____

_____

_____

_____

_____

_____

_____

My Prayer Requests

My Praise Reports

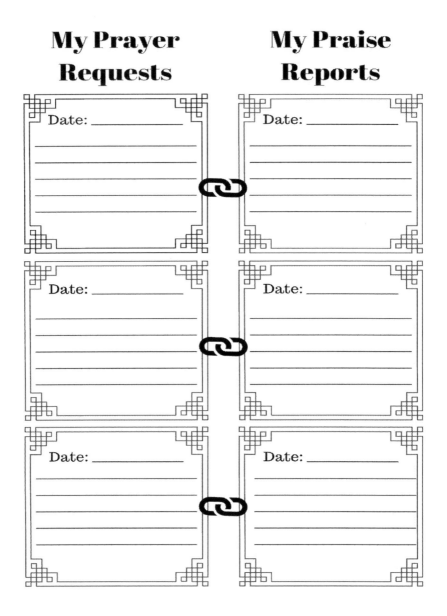

Date: _____

Date: _____

Date: _____

Date: _____

Date: _____

Date: _____

Note Page

_____

_____

_____

_____

_____

_____

_____

_____

_____

_____

_____

_____

_____

_____

_____

_____

_____

_____

_____

_____

_____

_____

_____

_____

_____

_____

_____

My Prayer Requests

My Praise Reports

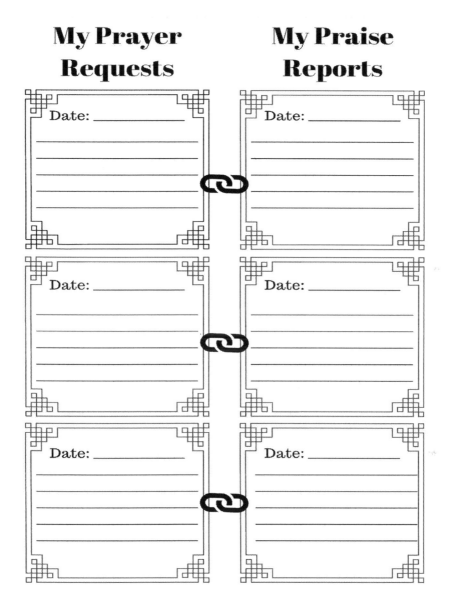

Date: _____

Date: _____

Date: _____

Date: _____

Date: _____

Date: _____

Note Page

_____

_____

_____

_____

_____

_____

_____

_____

_____

_____

_____

_____

_____

_____

_____

_____

_____

_____

_____

_____

_____

_____

_____

_____

_____

1 John 5:14

"This is the confidence
we have in
approaching God:
that if we ask
anything according
to his will,
he hears us."

What is your favorite Bible story?

_____

_____

_____

_____

My Prayer Requests

My Praise Reports

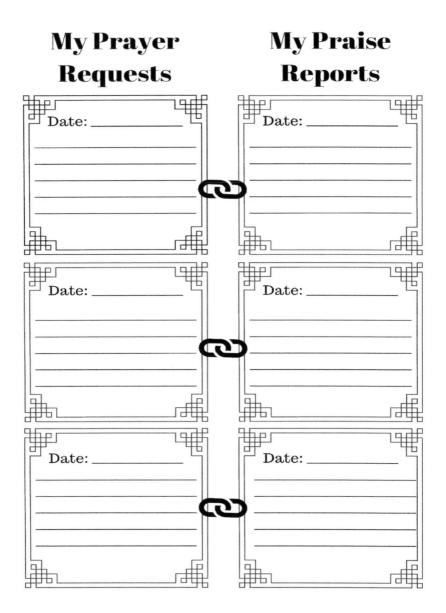

Date: _____

Date: _____

Date: _____

Date: _____

Date: _____

Date: _____

Note Page

_____

_____

_____

_____

_____

_____

_____

_____

_____

_____

_____

_____

_____

_____

_____

_____

_____

_____

_____

_____

_____

_____

_____

_____

_____

_____

_____

My Prayer Requests

My Praise Reports

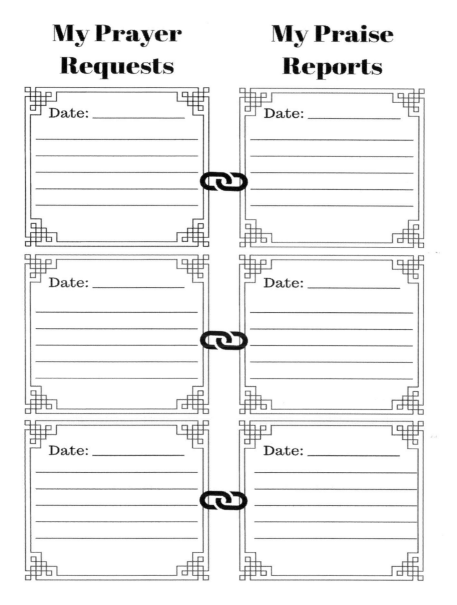

Date: _____

Date: _____

Date: _____

Date: _____

Date: _____

Date: _____

Note Page

_____

_____

_____

_____

_____

_____

_____

_____

_____

_____

_____

_____

_____

_____

_____

_____

_____

_____

_____

_____

_____

_____

_____

_____

_____

_____

_____

My Prayer Requests

My Praise Reports

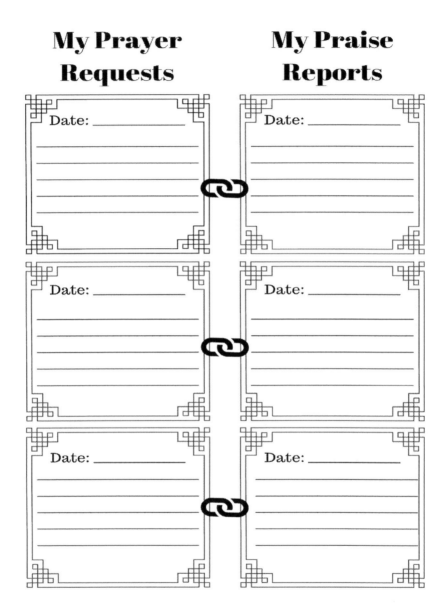

Date: _____

Date: _____

Date: _____

Date: _____

Date: _____

Date: _____

Note Page

_____

_____

_____

_____

_____

_____

_____

_____

_____

_____

_____

_____

_____

_____

_____

_____

_____

_____

_____

_____

_____

_____

_____

_____

_____

_____

_____

_____

_____

My Prayer Requests   My Praise Reports

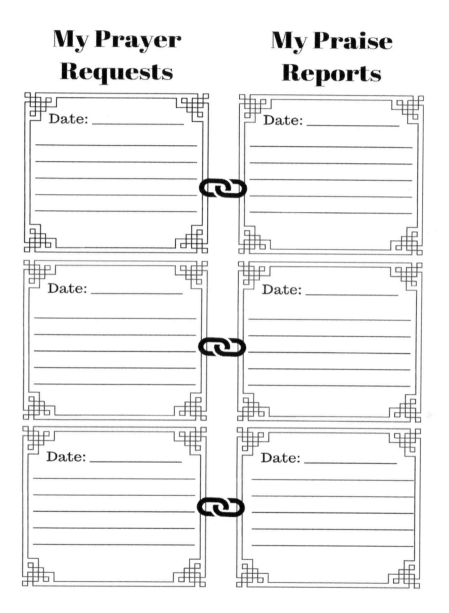

Date: _____

Date: _____

Date: _____

Date: _____

Date: _____

Date: _____

Note Page

_____

_____

_____

_____

_____

_____

_____

_____

_____

_____

_____

_____

_____

_____

_____

_____

_____

_____

_____

_____

_____

_____

_____

_____

_____

_____

My Prayer Requests

My Praise Reports

Date: _____

Date: _____

Date: _____

Date: _____

Date: _____

Date: _____

Note Page

_____

_____

_____

_____

_____

_____

_____

_____

_____

_____

_____

_____

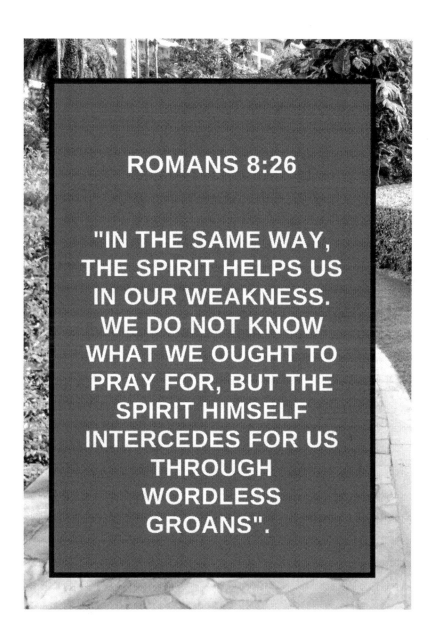

ROMANS 8:26

"IN THE SAME WAY, THE SPIRIT HELPS US IN OUR WEAKNESS. WE DO NOT KNOW WHAT WE OUGHT TO PRAY FOR, BUT THE SPIRIT HIMSELF INTERCEDES FOR US THROUGH WORDLESS GROANS".

FAithful

What is one thing that you are faithful in doing for your spiritual growth?

_____

_____

_____

_____

My Prayer Requests

My Praise Reports

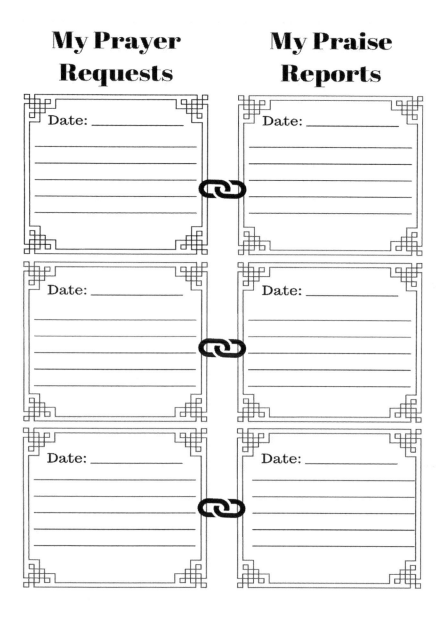

Date: _____

Date: _____

Date: _____

Date: _____

Date: _____

Date: _____

Prayer -N- Praise Diary

Note Page

_____

_____

_____

_____

_____

_____

_____

_____

_____

_____

_____

_____

_____

_____

_____

_____

_____

_____

_____

_____

_____

_____

_____

_____

_____

_____

My Prayer Requests

My Praise Reports

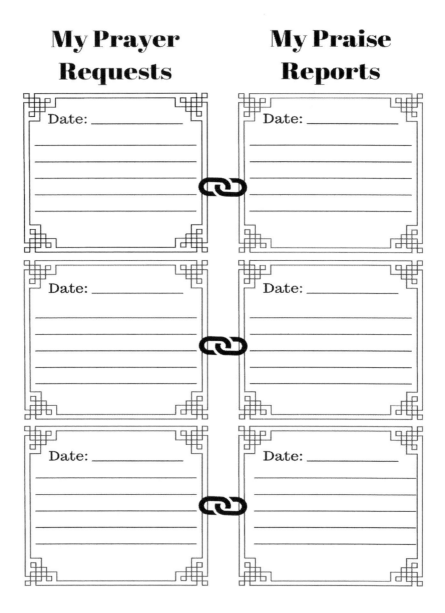

Date: _____

_____
_____
_____
_____
_____

Date: _____

_____
_____
_____
_____
_____

Date: _____

_____
_____
_____
_____
_____

Date: _____

_____
_____
_____
_____
_____

Date: _____

_____
_____
_____
_____
_____

Date: _____

_____
_____
_____
_____
_____

Note Page

_____

_____

_____

_____

_____

_____

_____

_____

_____

_____

_____

_____

_____

_____

_____

_____

_____

_____

_____

_____

_____

_____

_____

_____

_____

_____

_____

_____

My Prayer Requests

My Praise Reports

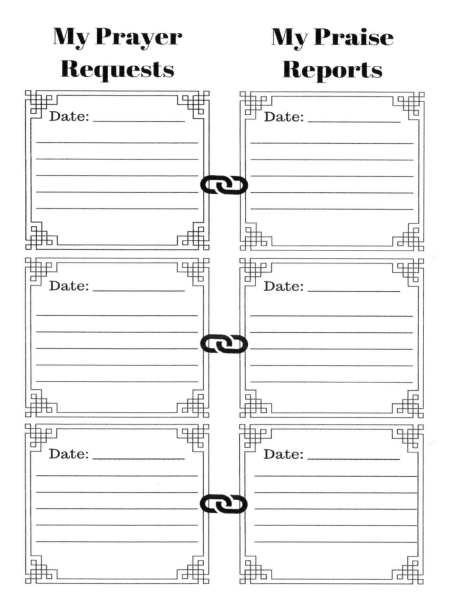

Date: _____

Date: _____

Date: _____

Date: _____

Date: _____

Date: _____

Note Page

_____

_____

_____

_____

_____

_____

_____

_____

_____

_____

_____

_____

_____

_____

My Prayer Requests   My Praise Reports

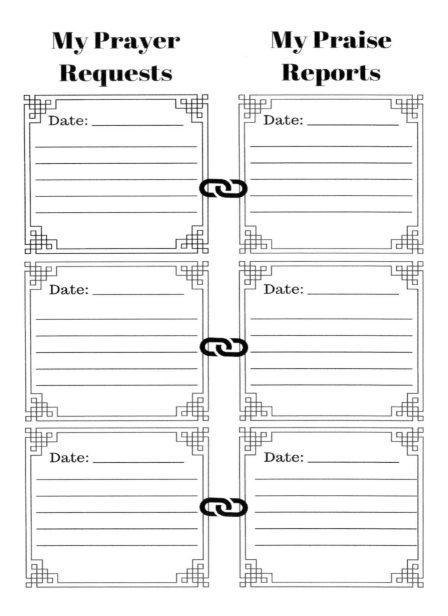

Note Page

_____

_____

_____

_____

_____

_____

_____

_____

_____

_____

_____

_____

_____

_____

_____

_____

_____

_____

_____

_____

_____

_____

_____

_____

_____

_____

_____

_____

_____

My Prayer Requests

My Praise Reports

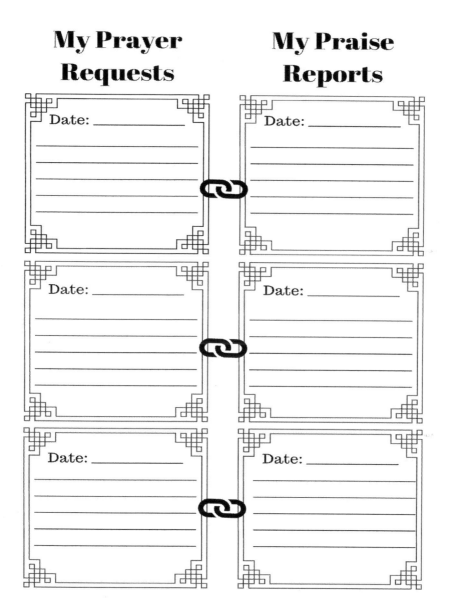

Date: _____

Date: _____

Date: _____

Date: _____

Date: _____

Date: _____

Note Page

_____

_____

_____

_____

_____

_____

_____

_____

_____

_____

_____

_____

Prayer -N- Praise Diary

_____

_____

_____

_____

_____

_____

_____

_____

_____

_____

_____

_____

_____

_____

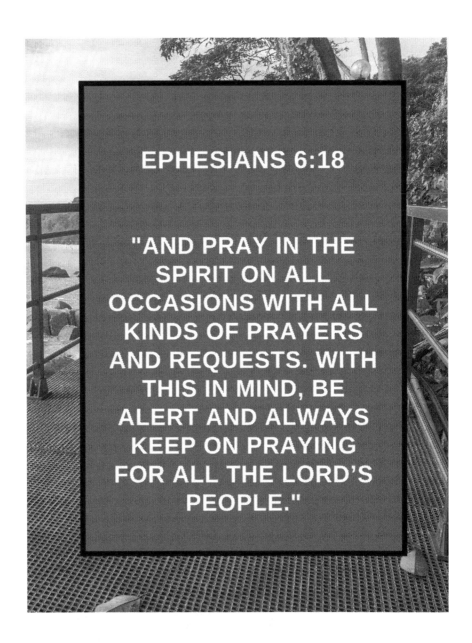

What about heaven are you most excited for?

_____

_____

_____

_____

My Prayer Requests

My Praise Reports

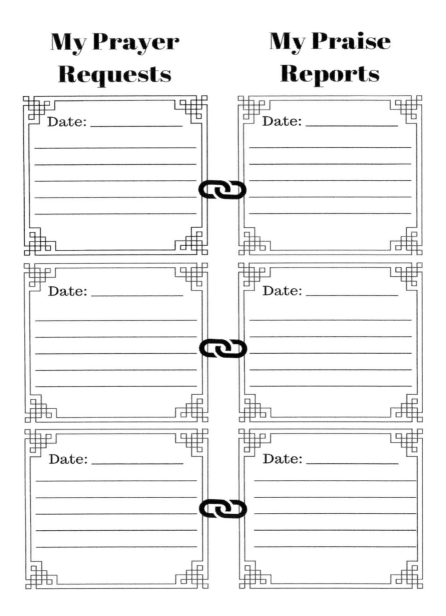

Date: _____

Date: _____

Date: _____

Date: _____

Date: _____

Date: _____

Note Page

_____

_____

_____

_____

_____

_____

_____

_____

_____

_____

_____

_____

_____

_____

_____

_____

_____

_____

_____

_____

_____

_____

_____

_____

_____

_____

_____

My Prayer Requests

My Praise Reports

Date: _____

Date: _____

Date: _____

Date: _____

Date: _____

Date: _____

Note Page

_____

_____

_____

_____

_____

_____

_____

_____

_____

_____

_____

_____

_____

Prayer -N- Praise Diary

_____

_____

_____

_____

_____

_____

_____

_____

_____

_____

_____

_____

_____

_____

My Prayer Requests

My Praise Reports

Date: _____

Date: _____

Date: _____

Date: _____

Date: _____

Date: _____

Note Page

_____

_____

_____

_____

_____

_____

_____

_____

_____

_____

_____

_____

_____

_____

_____

_____

_____

_____

_____

_____

_____

_____

_____

_____

_____

_____

_____

_____

_____

My Prayer Requests

My Praise Reports

Date: _____

Date: _____

Date: _____

Date: _____

Date: _____

Date: _____

Note Page

_____

_____

_____

_____

_____

_____

_____

_____

_____

_____

_____

_____

_____

My Prayer Requests

My Praise Reports

Date: _____

Date: _____

Date: _____

Date: _____

Date: _____

Date: _____

Note Page

_____

_____

_____

_____

_____

_____

_____

_____

_____

_____

_____

_____

_____

_____

_____

_____

_____

_____

_____

_____

_____

_____

_____

_____

_____

_____

_____

_____

_____

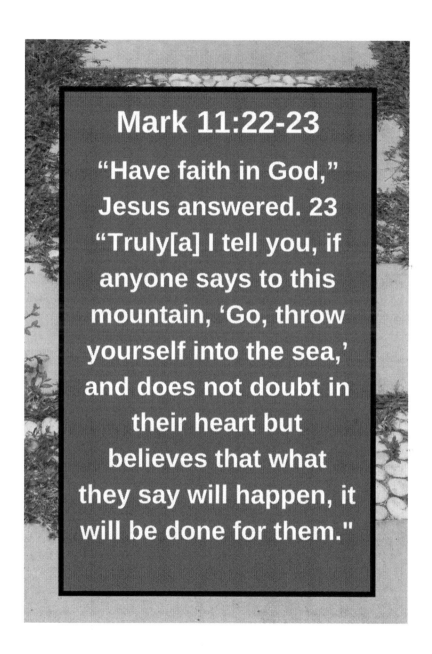

Mark 11:22-23

"Have faith in God," Jesus answered. 23 "Truly[a] I tell you, if anyone says to this mountain, 'Go, throw yourself into the sea,' and does not doubt in their heart but believes that what they say will happen, it will be done for them."

List one blessings God recently gave you:

_____

_____

_____

_____

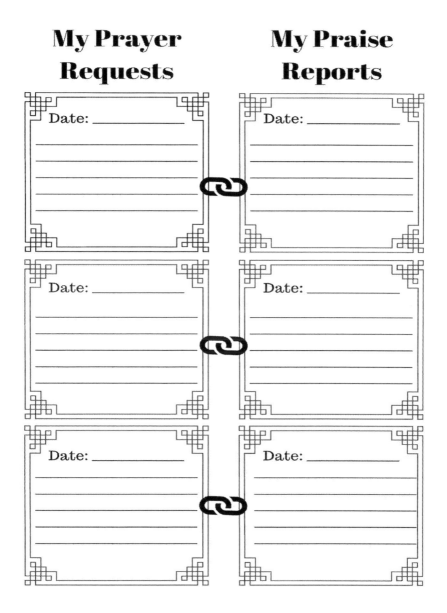

My Prayer Requests

My Praise Reports

Date: _____

Date: _____

Date: _____

Date: _____

Date: _____

Date: _____

Prayer -N- Praise Diary

Note Page

_____

_____

_____

_____

_____

_____

_____

_____

_____

_____

_____

_____

_____

_____

Prayer -N- Praise Diary

_____

_____

_____

_____

_____

_____

_____

_____

_____

_____

_____

_____

_____

_____

My Prayer Requests

My Praise Reports

Date: _____

_____
_____
_____
_____

Date: _____

_____
_____
_____
_____

Date: _____

_____
_____
_____
_____

Date: _____

_____
_____
_____
_____

Date: _____

_____
_____
_____
_____

Date: _____

_____
_____
_____
_____

Note Page

Prayer -N- Praise Diary

_____

_____

_____

_____

_____

_____

_____

_____

_____

_____

_____

_____

_____

My Prayer Requests

My Praise Reports

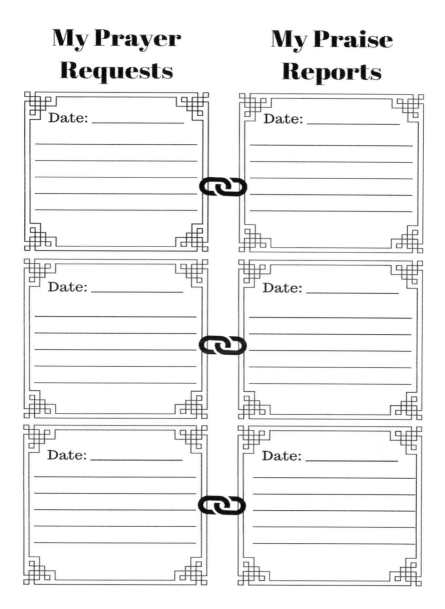

Date: _____

Date: _____

Date: _____

Date: _____

Date: _____

Date: _____

Note Page

_____

_____

_____

_____

_____

_____

_____

_____

_____

_____

_____

_____

_____

Prayer -N- Praise Diary

_____

_____

_____

_____

_____

_____

_____

_____

_____

_____

_____

_____

_____

_____

My Prayer Requests

My Praise Reports

Date: _____

Date: _____

Date: _____

Date: _____

Date: _____

Date: _____

Note Page

_____

_____

_____

_____

_____

_____

_____

_____

_____

_____

_____

_____

_____

_____

_____

_____

_____

_____

_____

_____

_____

_____

_____

_____

_____

_____

_____

_____

My Prayer Requests

My Praise Reports

Date: _____

Date: _____

Date: _____

Date: _____

Date: _____

Date: _____

Note Page

_____

_____

_____

_____

_____

_____

_____

_____

_____

_____

_____

_____

_____

_____

_____

_____

_____

_____

_____

_____

_____

_____

_____

_____

_____

_____

_____

ROMANS 12:12

"BE JOYFUL IN HOPE, PATIENT IN AFFLICTION, FAITHFUL IN PRAYER."

Color the word(s) that you feel today:

Brave

Encouraged

Motivated

Hopeful

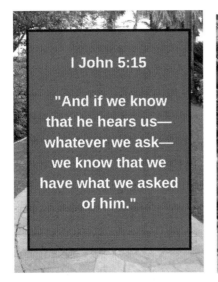

I John 5:15

"And if we know that he hears us— whatever we ask— we know that we have what we asked of him."

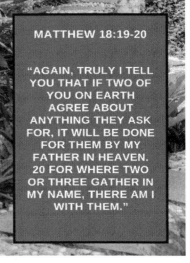

MATTHEW 18:19-20

"AGAIN, TRULY I TELL YOU THAT IF TWO OF YOU ON EARTH AGREE ABOUT ANYTHING THEY ASK FOR, IT WILL BE DONE FOR THEM BY MY FATHER IN HEAVEN. 20 FOR WHERE TWO OR THREE GATHER IN MY NAME, THERE AM I WITH THEM."

Mark 11:24-25

"Therefore I tell you, whatever you ask for in prayer, believe that you have received it, and it will be yours. And when you stand praying, if you hold anything against anyone, forgive them, so that your Father in heaven may forgive you your sins."

Matthew 6:7-8

"And when you pray, do not keep on babbling like pagans, for they think they will be heard because of their many words. Do not be like them, for your Father knows what you need before you ask him."

About Deidre

Deidre Proctor, Certified Business, Clarity and Accountability Coach, is the CEO of Deidre Proctor & Associates, LLC. She is also a Speaker, #1 Best-Selling Author, Philanthropist, Mentor, and Ministry Leader.

She is the author of "Great Before Birth-How To Harness The Power of God's DNA For An Extraordinary Life", the "Clarity To Success Journal", and Co-Author of "Black Women Speak Out, Stories of Racial Injustice in American".

www.deidreproctor.com

With over 20 years of experience in sales, sales training, marketing, and strategy development, Deidre's passion for helping others to achieve their goals has made her a highly sought-after Business Coach and Mentor to women who desire clarity in finding their purpose and those who have goals of starting their own business. She also created the Systematic Success Strategy For Female Entrepreneurs™. Deidre realized earlier on that she best fulfills her destiny when she helps others grow.

She is the Co-Founder and the CEO of Amazing Retreats International, LLC. Through their annual signature retreat, The Breathe Retreat, she has brought together Christian women from all walks of life that simply need a break from the hustle and bustle of life. This retreat is only for women who are ready to be refreshed, refocused, and rejuvenated with no distractions from home life or work life. The Breathe Retreat as sold out since it's 2015 conception, praise God!

Deidre is also the Founder and CEO of SHARE YOUR GENIUS. SYG is a group of businesswomen, entrepreneurs, and Ministry Leaders (current, retired, or aspiring), that support each other by sharing the unique skills and talents God has equipped us with. This support includes clarity, mindset, inspiration, empowerment, strategy, and accountability.

Deidre has been featured in media platforms such as Voyage Dallas Magazine, Xcellence Magazine, Heart and Soul Magazine, Glamher Magazine, Girlfriends Gathering Magazine, North Dallas Gazette, Lavida News/The Black Voice and various seminars, podcasts, and radio stations guest.

Deidre loves creating online courses, reading, and taking road trips with her husband. She is a Wife, Mother, and Grandmother. She and her husband reside in Texas.

For more information, or to follow Deidre please visit:
https://www.deidreproctor.com

https://www.instagram.com/coachdeidreproctor/

https://www.facebook.com/clarityandaccountabilitycoach/

https://shareyourgenius.org

Made in the USA
Columbia, SC
02 September 2022

66001776R00091